THE GEOGRAPHICAL ASSOCIATION

AWARENESS INTO ACTION

Environmental education in the primary curriculum

Bill Chambers

**with contributions from
Jane Featherstone and
Graham Ranger**

**The Geographical Association
Environmental Education Working
Group**

Series editor: Margaret Smeaton

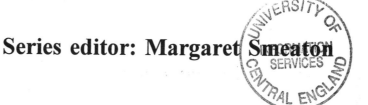

Acknowledgements

The authors and publishers are grateful to the following for permission to include copyright material:

Abbey Hey Infant School for the information on pages 18-19;
Bethesda School and Adele McNicol (now a teacher at Bridge College, Offerton, Stockport) for the information on pages 13 and 21-22;
Cheshire County Council Education Services Group for the flow chart on page 27;
Curriculum Council for Wales for the information on pages 6-8;
SCAA for the table on page 29;
Schofield and Sims for the worksheet on page 43;
The Tidy Britain Group for the figures on pages 4 and 25;

Edited by: Sue Greig
Text design: Chris Hand Design for Print
Cover design: Ledgard Jepson Ltd
Cover photos: Bill Chambers and Graham Ranger
Printed and bound in England by Watkiss Studios Ltd

ISBN 0 948512 95 4

The views expressed in this publication are those of the authors and do not necessarily represent those of the Geographical Association.

Published by the Geographical Association, 343 Fulwood Road, Sheffield S10 3BP. The Publications Officer of the GA would be happy to hear from other potential authors who have ideas for geography books. You may contact the Publications Officer via the GA at the address above.

The Geographical Association is a registered charity - no: 313129.

Contents

The what and why of environmental education

What is environmental education?

Environmental education is not about adding more content to an already overloaded curriculum. Rather, it is 'a whole dimension to education which may be thought of as an approach to learning' (CEE 1992). In today's society it is a vital perspective on the world. At its best it may change attitudes, values, beliefs and, most importantly, actions. At its worst it is the mindless litter pick or pond dip.

As you will see from the definitions below, there is wide agreement that environmental education should go far beyond basics, such as ecological processes and the identification of plants and animals, to include the development of a broad range of life skills, together with the exploration of attitudes and values.

Some definitions of environmental education

Environmental education has four overlapping components: curiosity and awareness about the environment; knowledge and understanding; skills; informed concern (*Environmental Education from 5 to 16*, HMI, 1989).

Environmental education is part of history, of geography, of science, of economic awareness: it catches us at every turn. It is a moral as well as a political issue and it may be concerned with social justice (Annual Review of Environmental Education, Presidential Address by Professor Tim Brighouse, 1989).

... learning situations which develop the sort of attitudes which will lead to concern for the welfare of environment and community ... (Project Environment, Schools Council, 1974).

Environmental Education is essentially conservation or applied ecology (Countryside Conference, Keele University, 1965).

... instilling in the minds and hearts of ... young people the understanding and commitment necessary to use the natural resources of this country successfully (*Imperatives in Education*, American Association of School Administrators, 1966).

Environmental education should encourage pleasure, curiosity and wonder in environmental work in urban areas (*Environmental Education in Urban Areas*, Department of the Environment, 1979).

continued...

About, in and for

A useful definition of environmental education is education about the environment, in the environment and for the environment. Education about the environment is concerned with environmental knowledge and understanding. Education in the environment is concerned with using it as resource for enquiry, the development of skills and direct experience. Education for the environment is concerned with the development of values and attitudes, such that direct and positive action, based on a broad, balanced and informed concern, may be taken.

Education about the environment

Curriculum Guidance 7: Environmental Education (NCC 1990c) lists the following seven topic areas through which a knowledge and understanding of the environment can be developed: climate; soils, rocks and minerals; water; energy; plants and animals; people and their communities; buildings, industrialisation and waste. It also provides a number of useful case studies, as does *Opening Doors for Science* (ASE 1990). For key stages 1 and 2 case studies described include 'The Nature Trail', 'The Gassing of Badgers' (NCC 1990c) and 'Visiting a Farm' and 'Litter and Rubbish' (ASE 1990).

The Curriculum Council for Wales (1992) approaches the content of environmental education through the identification of three key areas for environmental learning, and gives a comprehensive list of ideas and concepts associated with each.

Key areas for environmental education

Systems and interdependencies

The world is a complex network of interconnected and interdependent systems (ecological, physico-chemical, geological). Human societies, institutions, systems and cultures are integral components of these global systems.

continued...

Some examples of associated concepts and ideas:

- interplay between events and actions on local, regional and global scales;
- causes and effects, decisions and consequences;
- ecosystems, plants, animals and non-living environment depend upon and affect each other;
- energy sources and systems;
- relationships between humans and their environment - human impact on ecological systems and environmental effects on human societies;
- interdependence of the health of planet and people;
- repercussions of human actions or choices on quality of environments and communities.

Change and development

Environmental change through time occurs partly by natural processes and increasingly as a result of processes induced by human development - social, economic and technological.

Some examples of associated concepts and ideas:

- natural processes causing environmental change, past and present;
- effects of human activities (agriculture, economic growth, industrialisation, technology in general, leisure activities, consumerism, ...);
- climate changes and their causes;
- effects of differing or changing views about the earth, nature and environment;
- influence of past decisions and actions on the present;
- influence of environmental design on landscapes;
- interplay between environment and major influences on the physical environment;
- possible futures for planet, biosphere and people.

Sustainability and stewardship

Humans are necessarily consumers of the earth's resources but they carry a major responsibility for maintaining the well-being of the planet and all its inhabitants, human and non-human.

Some examples of associated concepts and ideas:

- types of resources (material, energy, renewable and non-renewable);
- sustainable management of resources;
- use of traditional/indigenous knowledge, skills and perceptions to live sustainably;
- recycling resources and reducing consumption;

continued...

- preventing pollution of air, sources and supplies of water, soil, seas and oceans;
- conservation of aspects of the environment;
- resolving conflicts of interest or need, e.g. between conservation/ environmental protection and human need for employment; or between use of renewable energy sources and aesthetic effects on landscapes;
- environmental responsibilities of governments, industry and citizens;
- development and implementation of legislation for the environment;
- effects of gender, culture and economic status on responses to environmental problems;
- alternative models for economic development;
- sustainable and 'organic' agriculture;
- appropriate technology (for both 'industrial' and 'developing' countries).

Source: Curriculum Council for Wales (1992).

Education in the environment

All good environmental education involves activities in the real world. It is concerned not only with the natural and rural world, but also with the human and urban. It is important for children to experience rural and urban, coastal and inland, lowland and upland, spoilt and unspoilt, and reclaimed and conserved environments as they grow up. The emphasis on the contrasting locality in primary geography reflects this entitlement.

In addition children should work out concentrically from the classroom to the school, the grounds, the locality, a contrasting locality and (either first hand or second hand) to distant environments.

The reality of work in the environment is very different from classroom theory. There are the distractions of noise, wind and other people, and the complexity of the real world to contend with. However study in the environment brings issues linking people and their environment alive, and thus offers a tangible context in which children can develop their ideas about and concern for the environment.

Education for the environment

A key concern of environmental education is care for the environment. Education for the environment gives pupils the opportunity to explore their personal responses to the environment and environmental issues, and to nurture individual attitudes and values. However, knowledge, understanding, awareness, attitudes and values without a commitment to action are of little value to individuals, society or the environment. Children should be encouraged to move from 'awareness to action'. To be truly worthwhile environmental education should have the potential to change behaviour. The process may not be more important than the product.

Most environmental actions seek either to reduce the problem directly or to raise awareness and motivation for action in others. An example of the first would be setting up a school paper recycling scheme, and of the second, writing to politicians or designing and displaying campaigning posters.

Why do environmental education?

Environmental education is about helping young people to understand the environmental issues all around them; to value their own as well as other (contrasting) environments; and to appreciate the role they can play in decision-making about the environment. Environmental education stresses the active and positive involvement and empowerment of individuals and groups of young people as well as governments, industrialists and politicians. However, it recognises that children should not be forced to feel guilty for all the woes of society, nor have totally naive faith in the power of the democratic process.

At a time of accelerating environmental decline, as a result of economic growth, industrial expansion, human population increase and higher levels of consumption, it is vital that the key issues affecting our planet are addressed through the school curriculum. Children in the 1990s are more environmentally aware than ever before. If we are to build on this concern and enthusiasm we must focus on finding answers to environmental problems, rather than simply identifying them. Environmental education is not only about pollution and extinction, but also about environmental successes due to human determination, resourcefulness and adaptability. Above all, environmental education can offer children themselves opportunities to take part in successful actions, however small, to protect and improve the environment.

In terms of the school curriculum, environmental education may be justified:

* as a cross-curricular theme that helps to give natural links and coherence to subject-led topics;
* as an approach to teaching and learning, not more content;
* as an area to which all subjects can contribute, if teaching and learning are designed to develop environmental awareness, understanding and the potential to take action;
* as an approach, which, if fully adopted, can enhance whole school management, ethos and culture, and positively affect the school's resource use and environmental impact.

Environmental education across the curriculum

Core and foundation subjects

Geography has a central role to play in the delivery of environmental education. Through the study of places, the human and physical processes which shape them and the people who live in them, geography helps children make sense of their surroundings and the wider world. It is not surprising then that the seven environmental topics listed in *Curriculum Guidance 7: Environmental Education* (NCC 1990c) are all to be found in the geography Orders. There are also several explicit references to the environment in the Geography National Curriculum for key stages 1 and 2 (NCC 1995).

At key stage 1 children are required to have opportunities to investigate, not only two localities (that of the school and of a contrasting area in the UK or overseas), but also 'the quality of the environment' in a locality. They are invited to express their likes and dislikes about the environment concerned, and to consider 'how that environment is changing', and 'how the quality of that environment might be sustained or improved'.

At key stage 2 in their study of places, pupils are required to be taught about 'environmental issues that give localities their character'. The geographical theme of environmental change at key stage 2 requires children to be taught 'how people affect the environment', and 'how and why people seek to manage and sustain their environment'.

In addition, the key stage 2 theme, settlement, refers to the study of 'a particular issue arising from the way land is used', the example given being one of conflicting views on the construction of a by-pass.

Environmental issues take place in geographical locations and frequently cross national frontiers. The interdependence of environmental education and geography is illustrated by the following extract taken from the Northumberland County Council guidelines for environmental education:

> The Geography National Curriculum with its distinctive concern for area studies at a range of scales from local to global is particularly relevant for Environmental Education. Where environmental issues are concerned national boundaries are of little importance. The problems of global warming and acid rain cannot be solved by any one country. This is also true for the problems caused by mass tourism; the Alps for example, form part of our European heritage and their protection requires co-operation on an international scale. Pupils should therefore be helped to understand the relationships between countries in terms of space, resources and the effects of their activities on each other (Northumberland County Council, undated).

However environmental education should not be thought of as just an extension of geography. Environmental issues have wide cross-curricular relevance. Furthermore involvement in issues or actions to protect or improve the environment has not traditionally been a part of geography or indeed of any other curriculum subject.

> Each subject area explores different aspects of human understanding and experience and each subject can be used to help pupils develop insights into human behaviour and its effects on the environment. A programme for environmental education which draws on the whole curriculum will give pupils the opportunity to consider environmental issues from the perspectives mentioned earlier - physical, geographical, biological, sociological, economic, political, technological, aesthetic, ethical and spiritual (NCC 1990c).

Several attempts have been made to identify the environmental content of each core and foundation subject, through the listing of specific attainment targets (NCC 1990c; Council for Environmental Education 1992). Several local education authority guidelines offer in-depth analysis (e.g. Northumberland County Council, undated; Sefton Local Education Authority, 1994). Birmingham City Council (1992) and the Curriculum Council for Wales (1992) have also produced matrices.

Subsequent changes to the National Curriculum mean that some of these documents, whilst still offering guidance, are now less useful. The table below from Pike and Selby (1990) suggests more general ways in which various subjects can contribute to environmental education.

Environmental education across the curriculum

English
- stories, novels, plays and poems from around the world on environmental themes
- drama and role play to elucidate attitudes and perspectives on environmental issues
- comprehension, creative writing and discussion around environmental topics to develop reflective and language skills
- media studies programmes based around environmental films

Mathematics
- interpreting statistics on environmental trends and developments
- developing basic mathematical skills through case study work on the local environment
- understanding, estimating and calculating probabilities using contemporary environmental data
- calculating distances, lengths and angles using the natural and built environments

continued...

Science
- chemical changes to the earth's atmosphere caused by human and industrial activity
- the physics of energy production from renewable and non-renewable resources and their environmental impact
- food webs and ecosystems and the impact of inorganic fertilizers, pesticides and waste products
- the science of global warming

Technology
- planning and developing environmentally-friendly technologies
- identifying student's recreational needs and designing appropriate play equipment and environments
- selecting, retrieving and using data from an environmental data base
- using information technology to present environmental data in different forms

History/geography
- the harnessing of energy through the ages and its social, economic and environmental effects
- oral history projects explaining people's recollections of past environments
- developing a critical appreciation of the concepts of sustainable development, stewardship and conservation

Modern foreign languages
- using material on environmental issues for the practice and development of language skills
- exploring environmental topics from non-European countries where the language under study is spoken
- simple structured conversations around photographs depicting pleasing natural and built environments
- studying a local environment issue as part of a foreign language exchange programme

Creative and recreational arts
- drawing, painting and 3-D work to sensitise students to their environment
- composing, interpreting and performing music on environmental themes
- using theatre techniques to raise awareness of the controversial nature of many environmental issues
- appreciating the environment within outdoor activity programmes

Religious education
- perspectives of different world religions on the environment and particular environmental issues
- moral and ethical implications of political, social and economic decisions affecting the environment
- considering personal responsibility to all living things
- exploring green spirituality

Source: Pike and Selby (1990).

The Council for Environmental Education has produced a number of *Inset 5-16* packs, for English, science, geography, the arts, technology and initial teacher education, in which you will find an abundance of ideas and approaches to environmental education (CEE 1992, 1993, 1994a,b, 1995a,b).

In recent years outdoor education and religious education have also developed environmental education approaches. The emphasis of both is on attitudes and values, rather than knowledge and understanding. Care and concern for the environment, as well as recognition of beauty, are key elements. Manchester City Council, in conjunction with the Field Studies Council, have produced a guide linking outdoor and environmental education (MCC/FSC 1993). In 1994 the Religious Education and Environment Programme was founded with the conviction that concern for nature is essential to religion and that religious awareness has a vital contribution to make to respect for nature.

Environmental education and cross-curricular elements

The cross-curricular elements are the dimensions, skills and themes which bond the 'bricks' of the attainment targets and programmes of study of the basic curriculum into a 'cohesive structure' (NCC 1989). The dimensions involve the development of 'positive attitudes to gender equality, cultural diversity and special needs'. (NCC 1990a). Skills (communication, information technology, numeracy, personal and social, problem solving and study) are not subject or theme specific and are developed across the whole curriculum. The themes (Careers, Economic and Industrial Understanding, Citizenship, Health and Environmental Education) are 'less pervasive' than the dimensions and skills but the National Curriculum requires that the knowledge, skills and attitudinal objectives of each are delivered by schools in an appropriate manner. A number of LEAs have produced their own cross-curricular guidelines (e.g. Manchester 1991). The examples which follow illustrate how you can meet some of the curriculum requirements for the cross-curricular dimensions and themes through environmental education.

Gender equality and cultural diversity

The inclusion of a range of cultural and gender perspectives on the environment from this country and around the world can serve the complementary goals of environmental education and these two dimensions. You might choose for example to study women's role in the collection of water and firewood for energy in third world countries.

Parkside School undertook a project which linked geography and religious education with environmental education on a theme of 'Women and Development'. A unit of work was developed which met the requirements of the Geography Order to study a locality in an economically developing country and to link this with an investigation of the impact of wealth and environment on the lives of women. The lives of two women, both living in Kenya, but of different backgrounds were studied. One had access to education, health care and responsibility for her own fertility, the other did not. The factors leading to the disparity were investigated in order to attempt an understanding of why the lives of the two women were so different. The issue was seen to be one of gender and the role and perception of women in society. This project also successfully challenged stereotyped images of the uniformity of social conditions in countries such as Kenya.

Stanton-in-the-Peak Primary School helped develop the appreciation of cultural diversity at key stage 2 through the teaching of a contrasting locality. It twinned with a multicultural school and each school developed a sensory trail about the cultural environment of their own locality. By doing both their own trail and that of their partner school, everyone involved learned to value not only their own contributing culture but also that of others.

Special needs

Four groups of pupils are identified by the National Curriculum Council as having special needs; these are those with exceptionally severe learning difficulties associated with both behaviour and multi-sensory impairment, those with other learning difficulties, those with physical or sensory impairment and exceptionally able pupils. Environmental education can provide a context for active and positive involvement of all children in a wide range of activities.

At Bethesda School in Stockport a Wildlife Garden has recently been created which provides access for disabled pupils (see also pages 22-23). This conservation project has enabled the pupils to have first hand experiences to explore and discover the world around them. The project was designed after extensive discussions with pupils and staff and includes a terrace garden with access from each classroom, high-rise mini-beast homes, sensory areas, wildlife pond and a water feature, raised flower beds and tubs. The project has permeated every area of the curriculum and acted as a forum for many cross-curricular links with science, art, maths, design and technology, and English. It has provided excellent opportunities for meeting the demands of the National Curriculum and work has been developed especially in science to suit the individual needs of children working in key stages 1 and 2.

Bethesda pupils are being educated about their environment as they create habitats, green their surroundings, learn the importance of conservation, recycling and observe seasonal changes. They are learning through the medium of the Wildlife Garden which has stimulated much language development as they communicate their findings. The school is certain that the learning experiences the garden provides has reinforced positive values and attitudes about caring for the environment.

Ashgate Croft is a school for young people with physical and mental disabilities. Their ability to make sense of their environment and therefore their access to that environment is severely limited. In order to give these young people a measure of *independence, a programme of class activities and fieldwork has been developed by the humanities department. The investigation of an environmental issue concerned with access was used as a stimulus to skill and knowledge development. This has included activities to enable the pupils to make an assessment of the facilities of the town. They carried out an investigation to discover how well the town functions for people using wheelchairs or who have hearing or sight impairment.*

Careers education and guidance

By preparing pupils for the choices, changes and transitions affecting their future training and employment, careers education and guidance aims to enable young people to be effective in a variety of adult occupations and roles. Environmental education can help children learn about different kinds of work in their local area, and ways in which work in the locality has changed the environment. It can give them experience of work and may also challenge sex stereotyping.

At a time of recession and high unemployment, and especially in cities where pockets of unemployment can exceed 50 per cent, environmentalism may be seen as a luxury which we cannot afford. Add to this the widespread perception that environmentalism is anti-industry and can threaten jobs whilst safeguarding the rights of animals and plants, and there is potential for conflict. This need not be the case. Globally environmental well-being and social/economic well-being are increasingly seen as two sides of the same coin. In this country too there is growing recognition of the interconnectedness of environmental and social/economic problems, particularly in urban areas.

In inner city Liverpool, at Tiber Street School, environmental education and careers education are being used to help overcome the physical and socio-economic disadvantages affecting the children of the area. It is hoped that by improving the local environment and changing the children's perceptions of employment, real community development may be achieved. Environmental improvement and commitment has been addressed with the formation of a 'Litter Squad' to fight the degradation associated with the litter dropped in the school, its grounds and the locality. The squad has its own uniform and has received financial support from local industry. It has developed into a form of community service with aid regularly given to neighbouring old people's homes. Another aspect of the project is to challenge the negative self-perceptions of the children of the locality. Here particular attention has been paid to racial and gender disadvantage and stereotyping. Careers conventions for juniors, the presentation of positive role models for black and mixed race children and attempts to undermine gender employment stereotyping, have all been successfully introduced.

Citizenship

Citizenship is about helping pupils develop knowledge and understanding of the nature of community, roles and relationships in a democratic society and the nature and basis of duties, responsibilities and rights. In addition, citizenship is concerned with a range of attitudes, moral codes and values, the majority of which are directly relevant to environmental education (NCC 1990d). Through active participation in the life of the school and local community, children can experience, from a very early age, the role of responsible citizens. In many ways the aims of citizenship and environmental education coincide. Children need to have a sense of ownership of place, and to know, through direct experience, that they can improve their community and its environment. Schools can also act as models of participative democracy, where young people learn the skills and knowledge of the curriculum, as well as gaining the confidence to be environmentally active, concerned and responsible citizens.

In Gwent, the Blaina Heritage Group (in conjunction with Community Design for Gwent) was concerned to make young people in the area aware of their heritage and to regenerate a sense of community. This group of 70 to 80 year old retired miners learned new graphic design skills and made displays for their ever-growing exhibition. They also visited local secondary and primary schools to discuss the decline of their village and the alienation and lack of facilities for the young people of the area.

Economic and industrial understanding

For many years in the environmental movement there has been an antagonism towards industry and the industrial and economic growth ethic. Clear differences in philosophical and ethical positions have lead to feelings of incompatibility between the 'ecocentrists' and the 'technocentrists'. Conversely, environmental priorities have not been high on the agenda for most in industry. In recent years moderate environmentalists and some industrialists have realised that such confrontational antagonism is of little value to either group. These and other concerns about the marginalisation, unattractiveness, and perceived irrelevance of industry have lead to the inclusion of economic and industrial understanding in the National Curriculum. Links between schools, environment and industry have also been fostered by the establishment of such initiatives as the School Curriculum Industry Partnership (SCIP) and Groundwork's ESSO Greenlink Project.

Education for economic and industrial understanding aims to help pupils organise their own finances, to form views on economic and industrial issues and to prepare them for their present and future economic roles; as producers, consumers and citizens in a democracy (NCC 1990b). Clearly these aims, together with specific statements concerning the impact of economic activity and growth on the environment, and a variety of themes identified by teachers on INSET courses such as 'the impact on the local community of building a bypass', 'studying the production of energy and the environmental impact of different sources of energy' and 'investigating the implications of global warming and how society contributes to its build-up' (NCC 1991), have major relevance to environmental education.

The SCIP has produced fifteen simulations available to local education authorities subscribing to the SCIP/Mini-Enterprise in School Project under the Department of Trade and Industry Work Related Curriculum Initiative. These include the *Dustbin Game* which involves sorting 'contrived rubbish' and then discussing issues associated with waste, the morality of waste packaging, the economics of recycling, energy use in packing, production and biodegradability. Another pack in the same series *Industry and Environment - Friend or Foe?* examines the issue of selling toxic waste around the world.

In one of the pilot Greenlink projects, links between industry and schools on Merseyside were developed and many had environmental education (and geography) at the core. A tea importer, a seaweed to salad cream manufacturer, Kelloggs, Wimpey the Builders, and a hardwood timber importer were all involved in projects with an environmental dimension. For example, year 6 children examined the site and the product of Kellogg's Corn Mill at Seaforth Dock, Liverpool, and produced curriculum work on the environmental impact of the plant and process on the locality.

Health education

Environmental education offers opportunities to consider aspects of health education at the individual, group and community levels. By studying the school's environment children become aware of potential dangers and health hazards, and they are encouraged to take personal responsibility for the care of the school and other environments.

Liverpool LEA has in recent years promoted two interesting health-environment related activities.

St John Almond School took part in the European 'Healthy Cities' project with ten other European cities. Participating schools were encouraged to explore a theme relating to Healthy Cities and the particular health and environmental concerns of that school. A number of themes such as pollution, traffic, open spaces and drug abuse were generally considered, and in Liverpool specific studies were made of poor housing, recreation and leisure and diet and health care, as the factors affecting the current health of the city and the findings were then communicated to the partner school in Europe.

The School Meals Service has adopted a pro-active approach to marketing and healthy eating. This has involved the surveying of pupils as to their eating habits and preferences and a 'Healthy Eating' educational programme. Numerous competitions were sponsored and many schools participated in food and other health-related activities, including dental care.

How do you do environmental education?

For most schools environmental education is not an additional subject, but is delivered through the formal and/or informal curricula. To fulfil the pupils' entitlement you may find it necessary to integrate opportunities for environmental education across the subjects with other opportunities in the curriculum, within personal and social education for example, and within the wider community of which the school is a part.

The formal curriculum

Cross-curricular topic work

A wide range of environmental issues such as deforestation, a proposed by-pass or a new housing estate can provide a focus for integrated topic or theme work.

Abbey Hey Infant School in Manchester chose 'What a Load of Rubbish' as a whole school project to make the children more aware of caring for their immediate environment. The project was cross-curricular and allowed many opportunities for creative work, maths, language and scientific investigation. Activities ranged from collecting waste and turning it into musical instruments in the Nursery, to collage making, 'keeping our area tidy', to carrying out surveys and bottle recycling.

Abbey Hey Infant School

Whole School Topic

We chose this topic as a whole school project to make the children more aware of caring for their immediate environment, the importance of dealing with rubbish, and to some extent, how this is done.

The project was cross-curricular and allowed many opportunities for creative work, maths, language and scientific investigation.

Nursery: to collect a large selection of waste materials and then design and make musical instruments using appropriate material. Observation and discussion of materials before and after conversion.

Reception classes: children to collect materials and sort them into various properties. Creative writing and various methods of recording to be used. Make a collage 'Superclean'.

continued...

Middle infants: 'Keep our area tidy'. Scientific observation and investigation into litter and waste found in areas around the school canal area, Debdale Park, Gorton market and various entries and alleys. Collections and recording of findings.

Top infants: to use various methods of recording, e.g. graphs, surveys, to find out:

1. What have we thrown away today?
2. Which class has thrown away the most?
3. Survey of the school grounds.

What happens to rubbish? Where does it go?
Collection of bottles, use of bottle banks, recycling.

What should be done with rubbish?
Litter survey of the school grounds.
What have we thrown away today?
Which class has thrown away the most?
What happens to rubbish? Where does it go?
Collection of bottles - use of bottle banks.

Keep our area tidy
Observation, investigation and recording of waste materials found in:
a) Debdale Park
b) along a canal walk
c) on Gorton market
d) in alleys and back entries
Ways to improve our attitude to litter?
What happens to waste in water, soil or left open to the air?

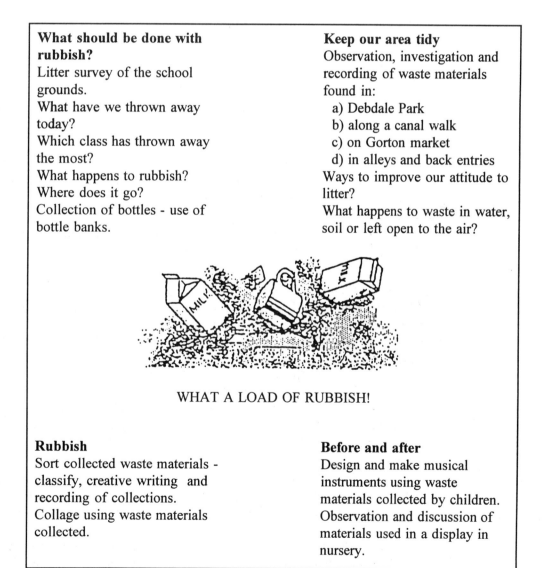

WHAT A LOAD OF RUBBISH!

Rubbish
Sort collected waste materials - classify, creative writing and recording of collections.
Collage using waste materials collected.

Before and after
Design and make musical instruments using waste materials collected by children. Observation and discussion of materials used in a display in nursery.

Even where the topics chosen are not obviously environmental in content, an environmental dimension or perspective can enhance the children's learning. For example the topic 'homes' could include pupils making an assessment of housing quality, or designing their ideal housing estate. Similarly the topic 'farms' could include the use of farms for conservation purposes or the ethics of factory farming.

Subject-specific work

Environmental issues can provide stimulating and relevant contexts for pupils' learning in a single subject such as science, geography, mathematics or English.

Osmanston School used a geography project to contribute to environmental education. They compared the use of land in their own village with that in the nearby town of Ashbourne. By asking the same enquiry questions of both localities, beginning with 'What is this place like?' and 'How is it changing?', children were able to map each area in the field, devise their own land use categories, work out the percentage of each land use cover in each place and describe the patterns of land use. This geographical work was extended into environmental education by involving the children in informed decision-making exercises which asked them to decide how each area should be developed and what impact on the environment would result.

At Wrythe Green Primary School in Sutton, the science co-ordinator organised a whole school exhibition called 'Science and the Environment'. Each class 3-11 year olds took part in a cross-curricular activity which combined science and the environment. Topics ranged from the Nursery Garden to our school, ourselves, building materials, living things, water, houses and weather, pollution, the ozone layer, sounds and the urban environment. All focused on helping the children explore, observe and care for the environment.

Special events

Since environmental education does not form part of the formal assessment process, except through the separate subjects, many schools favour its delivery through the enrichment week and day events. This allows a focus to be made, and you can make use of the enthusiasm of pupils, teachers, parents, local industries and dignitaries for a limited period of time. You may be able to synchronise a school environmental event with other local or national events, initiatives and competitions such as Environment Week, Industry Week or Riverwatch. Increasingly, you will find that funding, curriculum materials, personnel and sponsorship is available for such events. You should be prepared for the media attention which you may attract. Also you need to take care to avoid pitfalls, such as the criticism of tokenism and practical activities which are left unfinished or are unrelated to the curriculum.

Environment Week is sponsored by British Telecom and organised by the Civic Trust. It is a national event and takes place annually towards the end of May. It is unusual in being one of the few events held to celebrate the built environment.

British Telecom Awards are awarded to individuals, groups and organisations who take action to improve the quality of the places where people live and work. Local authorities and other organisations, including schools, plan local events as part of their contribution to Environment Week. Most years the weekdays are allocated to specific themes which have included the built environment, the green consumer, transport and the environment, and art in the environment. The weekends are often given to days of commitment where individuals make a pledge to take action to change their own lifestyles for the well-being of the environment and people.

During Environment Week 1993, the Merseyside Environment Trust advertised 83 events of which 15 were located in school grounds and some ten others involved school participation in the local community. Most popular activities were associated with tree, bush and wildflower planting, clean ups, pond digging and clearing and butterfly gardens, but others included the design of seating, path laying and fencing.

Residential and day centre fieldwork

Increasing numbers of schools are attempting to carry out much of their environmental education whilst on their annual residential field trip. This has many advantages for you the teacher:

- curriculum resources and equipment are usually available;
- there is more time to work with the children;
- specialist teacher-warden expertise is on hand;
- on-going project locations can be revisited from year to year;
- opportunities for fully integrated cross-curricular approaches are available.

However there a number of potential disadvantages to be aware of, when confining environmental education to one field experience. Have you abdicated responsibility to the centre and its wardens? Do the children take part in environmental activities at other times and places? Is all your environmental education rural-based?

At Colomendy, Liverpool LEA's centre in North Wales, many primary schools use the residential experience to cover some of their environmental education curriculum. Traditional geography themes such as the limestone quarry visit are being used increasingly for environmental purposes. Issues such as air, water and noise pollution and land use conflict based upon role plays, the use of resources from local newspapers and interviews with planners, local residents and quarry workers are commonly used, as well as fossil hunting and testing rocks with acid.

In addition to the residential experience, many centres offer structured day fieldwork. Throughout the country a network of Urban Studies Centres exists. These provide particular insight into the built environment, urban issues and planning. The Field Studies Council at Epping Forest offers a similar opportunity but in a rural environment, whilst a host of centres, including those operated by the National Trust, local authorities and industries, offer increasingly sophisticated resources appropriate for environmental education. City farms are widespread and provide useful experiences for urban children.

The informal curriculum

The informal curriculum provides educational opportunities for the development of both implicit and explicit environmental values and attitudes through extra-curricular activities and the hidden curriculum. Extra-curricular activities take place outside the formal curriculum either in or beyond the school, and with or without the personal supervision of teachers. They may make a very significant and memorable contribution to the educational experience of pupils. Environmental education activities and experiences may be very appropriate for this part of the whole curriculum.

The hidden curriculum is one of a range of 'contributory factors' which comprise all the implicit values that are transmitted, whether intentionally or not. Pupils cannot be expected to value things not valued by the school whether it be the school fabric and grounds, the inter-personal relationships between teachers and pupils, or teachers and ancillary staff and the attitude of the school to inequalities and injustice in the UK or overseas. These hidden values may manifest themselves in many ways including attitudes to charity, school assemblies, the involvement of parents and other adults, attitudes to animals and pets and to the use, reuse and conservation of resources.

Environmental award schemes

In many schools award schemes and competitions are part of the informal curriculum. Environmental award schemes stimulate and reward environmental action. In so doing they can offer opportunities to develop environmental education projects which have an action-focus. An example would be auditing the waste disposal facilities in a village and making recommendations to the parish council to resite and add more litter disposal facilities. You can run such schemes internally or externally. Internally children gain credits or points which lead to an award of some kind. Increasingly these awards are sponsored by industry, voluntary agencies, non-governmental organisations and charities.

It is important that such action schemes are used to increase environmental understanding. A school's decision to recycle its aluminium cans needs to be informed by an understanding of why recycling is necessary, what the alternatives are (drink less coke?) and what happens to recycled aluminium.

Witton Park School in Blackburn has an environmental awards scheme which promotes a series of environmental tasks that pupils can complete in and out of school. Each task gains a number of points which lead to the award of Bronze (100 points), Silver (350) and Gold (600) Award. As well as certificates, prizes are awarded to the highest scorer in each class and to the highest overall score. Tasks include joining a conservation group (50 points), writing an article for the school or local newspaper, making and using a bird table, having a car converted to unleaded petrol and helping wardens in a local country park.

Since 1989 Bethesda School in Cheadle has been developing its wildlife garden with access for disabled pupils. An important part of the project has been the

Bethesda Wild life Garden. '91

success in raising over £10,000 in environmental grants, awards, competitions and donations. In 1989 they won a Manchester Nature Conservation Award (£100) for their recycling guide. Since then they have won £1,000 with a Granada Landscape Award, £4,500 for a Blue Peter-Sainsbury's Green Scheme, £500 from the Midland Bank and £200 from Trust House Forte. Numerous other donations from the Friends of Bethesda, Cheadle Liberal Club and the local Round Table have also been received. Most recently they won the Queen's Jubilee Award. All this money has been used to improve the garden. Most recently a meandering path for wheelchairs has been built, linking the marsh area with other habitats created by the children.

(See page 14 for more information about Bethesda Wildlife Garden.)

Winners of the Tidy Britain Group 1993 Queen Mother's Birthday Awards for Environmental Improvement included Eastern County Primary School, Port Talbot. This school is sandwiched between the giant British Steel plant and the M4 motorway. Here, parents and pupils as part of the 'E' team created a 'secret garden'. Other activities include recycling, tree planting, composting and litter control. At Gateway Primary School in London the children, parents and local community combined to create a delightful green haven for the nursery pupils from the surrounding city estates.

English Nature School Grants Scheme aims to increase awareness of nature conservation issues among school children. English Nature gives grants to school projects working to achieve this end. For most schools this has meant that they have been helped to develop conservation areas in their grounds in order to provide an accessible natural resource for learning. Groundwork Trusts and Shell Better Britain also give funds to schools at the planning stage of such projects whilst the Learning Through Landscapes Trust acts as an advisory agency which also gives awards for completed projects in urban areas.

Trailblazer, a project developed by Nottinghamshire LEA, is a record of achievement scheme which gives pupils credit and recognition for their achievement in environmental education. It aims to encourage pupils to become independent learners through involvement in the processes of planning and evaluating experiences in the environment and the school. The principles of this LEA scheme could be adopted by any school as a means of recognising achievements in environmental education in the formal and informal curriculum.

Environment clubs

Clubs, whether for sport, music or stamp collecting have long formed an important and memorable part of the whole school informal curriculum. Environment clubs are a relatively recent addition. They may involve activities both within school at break and lunchtimes or after school or out of school but under the guidance of the teacher. The clubs maybe fully lead by the teacher or run with the assistance of parents and other interested adults. Alternatively the clubs may be at least resourced by outside organisations such as WATCH, the Royal Society for the Protection of Birds or Groundwork.

At Pex Hill, Knowsley Council Countryside Ranger Service run a Chrysalis Club for schoolchildren. This is affiliated to WATCH and meets bi-monthly on Saturdays and members are encouraged to help the rangers with various tasks and projects. In addition there are events to attend and excursions to local conservation sites of interest including all the country park facilities in the borough. Between five and 20 primary school children attend each session.

At the Sefton Coast Sand Dune system, a 'Natterjack Club', also affiliated to WATCH, meets once a month to carry out simple conservation tasks such as digging out toad scrapes, laying Christmas trees as brashing, visiting nearby bird reserves and organising recycling days. Sometimes they work on more dangerous and demanding tasks with (secondary) pupils on the Duke of Edinburgh Award Scheme.

Action projects

Positive action for the environment is encouraged in both the Geography Order and the environmental education guidance where activities 'designed to improve the local environment or place they have visited' and 'active participation in resolving environmental problems' are advocated. You may find that such action projects, involving working with conservation groups, local authority rangers and other environmentalists, are particularly educationally and environmentally rewarding.

Amongst the many benefits of action for the environment are that it:

*   makes the participants (pupils and teachers) feel good;
*   is reality not rhetoric;
*   places theory in a practical context thus making it meaningful;
*   is action-orientated and may lead to changes in behaviour;
*   involves the formal and informal curriculum;

- may introduce children to other adults;
- may give children an introduction to outside agencies.

However, you should beware of using children as 'skivvies' or giving tasks as punishment. Action for the environment without understanding is as bad as action without commitment and commitment without action.

In general you will find that action projects are most successful if:

- the tasks are small, discrete, tangible and capable of completion in the time allocated;
- they have a significant academic and intellectual relevance which is made clear to the participants;
- the children have appropriate clothing and equipment;
- the task is safe and carefully supervised;
- it can be assessed;
- the children want to do it and are given a choice.

Our Lady of the Assumption RC Junior School in Liverpool, following the interest of the Headteacher who was a committee member of the Gateacre (Civic) Society, undertook to spring clean the statue of Queen Victoria standing at the village crossroads. Warm water, soap suds and elbow grease were essential ingredients of this example of civic pride rewarded with a Civic Trust for the North West award.

Five primary schools in the suburbs of Liverpool are at present involved in a plastics recycling scheme involving a company in Runcorn. Regular monthly collections of waste plastic are made by the company and small financial rewards are being achieved by the schools. Despite problems of bleach stains from unrinsed bottles and safe storage, the scheme is successful, most notably from a curriculum point of view. Links have been made with the Local Authority recycling officer and the National Plastics Federation, curriculum materials have been developed, and close links forged between the schools and the recycling company. A certificate awarding ceremony at a local college attended by the City Recycling Officer was an important part of the project.

Groundwork Colne Valley in conjunction with Esso has developed the Young Energy Savers project with a number of primary schools in Berkshire. This aims to develop a successful school-based energy programme which enables children to learn about energy and energy conservation so that they will be motivated to implement practical energy saving measures both at school and at home.

At Formby on the Sefton Coast south of Southport, the Coastal Education Officer runs formal and informal environmental education projects. She has identified a wide range of actions for dunes appropriate for primary school children ranging from planting marram grass to fix the dunes, to laying bark mulch to prevent footpath erosion.

Promoting projects: the process

Any project will benefit from the active involvement not only of pupils, but also of Teachers, other school staff, governors and outside individuals and agencies. The Tidy Britain Group (Stephenson and Mares 1992) proposes the flowchart below, to help you involve your whole school in planning any site development.

Involving pupils flowchart

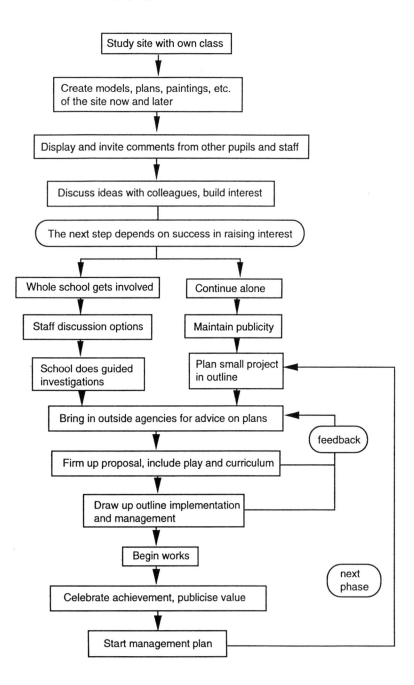

Source: Stephenson and Mares (1992), Tidy Britain Group.

You will also find it helpful to consider all the following factors when working towards a development plan for any environmental improvements:

- Governors' support.
- Grounds maintenance (contract obligations).
- Involving maximum number of pupils.
- Assessment and planning techniques (maps, surveys, models).
- County landscape architects (skills/resources).
- Maximising curriculum application.
- Broad teacher support.
- Sources of specialist advice.
- Making the most of process.
- Community involvement.
- Money, time, materials.
- Assessing the site: What have you got?.
- County architects' department (services and access).
- Democratic decision making.

Developing a long-term landscape plan

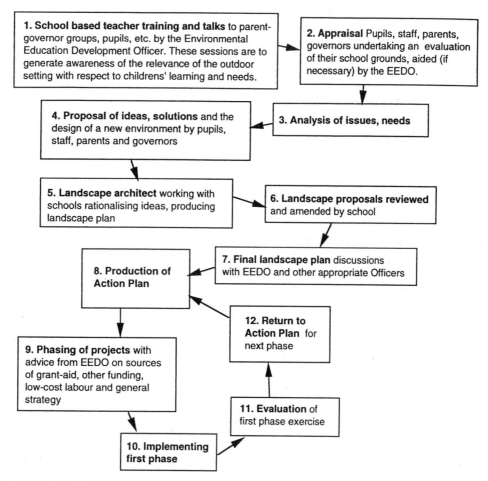

Reproduced by kind permission of Cheshire County Council Education Services Group.

Cheshire County Council (Stoker and Brawn 1993) produced a flowchart to guide Cheshire Schools through school grounds and landscape development projects. It is based upon successful practical experience and briefly sets out the procedure adopted by Cheshire Schools in establishing a long-term strategy.

Prior to such developments you may find it valuable to contact other organisations for financial, logistic or moral support. In 1993 the Merseyside Environment Trust, in conjunction with Liverpool City Council, held a conference for all organisations on Merseyside with an interest in the environment. At this a useful set of guidelines (see below) were provided to help promote a project.

Promoting a project

1. Know what you want to do. Have a clear idea of what the project is meant to achieve and be specific about the details - even to the point of having detailed building specifications if appropriate.

2. Believe in the project. Be determined that the project will succeed and take difficulties in your stride. Acts of vandalism or theft can be a good source of making everyone associated with the project more determined.

3. Be enthusiastic. Having a vision of what can be achieved is a great way of transferring enthusiasm for the scheme to others.

4. Let everybody become involved. Encourage everybody to make a contribution to the project and choose a project which has clear benefits for all.

5. Use the Press. Tell the local press and radio about the project - especially the local free press who love happy stories and community activity. Have a public launch of the project.

6. Approach sponsors. Approach companies who may be able to help in kind. Avoid asking for money. Explain the project and ask for any assistance possible. If your organisation is a school even the smallest of companies like to be making an input into the curriculum. This is an excellent way to obtain long term resources.
   Involve sponsors in updates on the project, give them feedback and make a special thank you.

7. Enter competitions. There are no losers in environmental competitions.

8. Keep an open door. Invite anyone and everyone to see what is going on; ward councillors, MP's, local people and businesses. If possible make the new facilities available to other community groups.

Source: Merseyside Environment Trust/Liverpool City Council (1993).

The enquiry and issues approaches

Enquiry

The enquiry approach is the basis for several of the National Curriculum core and foundation subjects including geography, science, design and technology and history. The 1991 Geography Orders stated that

> enquiry involves children in devising relevant questions, collecting and organising data and reaching a conclusion. It is a way of organising children's learning (and continues) ... to do this pupils need help with framing questions and require a rich source of supporting resources to enable them to collect data.

An enquiry does not have to be a major piece of work, it can be

> ... a short sequence of verbal questions and answers, as well as a longer piece of work involving research and the production of a written report.

In geography the whole curriculum is framed within an enquiry context, requiring

> studies that focus on geographical questions, e.g. What/where is it? What is it like? How did it get like this? (and, at key stage 2) How and why is it changing? (NCC 1995).

To carry out an enquiry you need to follow a clear enquiry sequence. Experimental and investigative science involves 'planning experimental work', 'obtaining evidence' and 'considering evidence'. In systematic enquiry at key stages 1 and 2 pupils are required to have opportunities to 'ask questions', 'use focused exploration and investigation to acquire scientific knowledge, understanding and skills' and to 'use both first-hand experience and simple secondary sources to obtain information' (NCC 1995).

The design and technology attainment targets, designing and making, are both set within an enquiry and problem solving context, whilst historical enquiry (asking and answering questions about the past) is a key element of the history programme of study at key stages 1 and 2 (NCC 1995).

The enquiry process in both theory and action is explored in *Teaching Geography at Key Stages 1 and 2: An INSET Guide* (NCC 1993). Here you will find some excellent examples of the enquiry process, associated with questions such as 'where can we find mini-beasts?', 'where shall we have a compass rose sited in our school grounds?', to the issue of whether a public house is an appropriate use of a piece of derelict land. Other examples include using weather data to answer questions such as 'which is the best site for a washing line?'. By using this approach you encourage the collection of data for a purpose, rather than for its own sake, and avoid the reassuring but meaningless 'if it moves, measure it' approach of many pupils. The enquiry process provides children with a meaningful focus for a project.

The enquiry process

Enquiry process in theory	Enquiry process in action in school grounds key stage 1
Recognise an issue or foc us for enquiry	Where shall we have a compass rose sited in our school grounds?
Ask some relevant questi ons or make a statement to be investigated (one or several as appropriate)	Should it be painted on tarmac, or bricks on the grass? In an open or exposed site? Near our classroom or not?
Collect relevant data	Check proposed sites for sun/shade - take wind, temperature judgements (for infants), measurements (for juniors). Check sites for flatness, drainage. Do a 'route' survey: would the proposed sites be in the official rights of way - on the football pitch?, or on the shortest route from the hall to another building?
Interpret and analyse data	Using data collected begin to decide on best location for compass rose
Present findings	Use plans, maps and diagrams to compare pros and cons of various sites
Draw conclusions	Decide on final siting - propose site to headteacher
Evaluate enquiry	See how well the actual site works out in practice - is it accessible/not too exposed? This would be monitored over a term or a year!

Source: *Teaching Geography at Key Stages 1 and 2*, NCC (1993).

Teachers at Malham Tarn Field Studies Centre, as part of a twenty day GEST course, were asked to carry out a physical enquiry which involved the use of simple equipment and the measurement of physical properties as specified in the Science and Geography orders. They were encouraged to pose questions associated with finding the best location for:

- *pitching a tent*
- *holding a barbecue*
- *fixing a bench*
- *a nature area*
- *reading the Sunday paper*
- *a picnic area*
- *playing badminton*
- *sunbathing*
- *storing the milk on a summer's day*

This created genuine interest and the collection of data associated with wind direction and velocity, air and ground temperature, light intensity, relative humidity, ground hardness, wetness, slope and irregularity. The importance of other non-physical variables such as distance, aesthetics, quality of the view, and human opinions and bias were discussed as was the whole concept of a fair test. All the measurements were related to a simple base map.

Issues

> There is a groundswell among young people of concern for the natural world. This is the foundation on which we can build a wider understanding of the issues (NCC 1990c).

An issue-based approach to the curriculum may be delivered through environmental education. Many contemporary issues have an environmental core, whether it be the disposal of nuclear waste, inner city degradation, car parking, tree felling, building on green space, the depletion of the ozone layer or global warming. However such issues are often controversial.

> ... environmental education is the subject of considerable debate and there is no clear consensus about many of the issues. This makes it all the more important to have opportunities at school to learn the facts about the environment, to develop a respect for evidence, to clarify their own values in relation to the environment and to understand that people hold different, equally legitimate points of view. Some of the issues are controversial and it is important that they are presented to pupils in a balanced way, which recognises all the points of view (NCC 1990c).

Some teachers are concerned about the controversial nature of many environmental issues. Whatever the issue there is a clear need to handle it in a balanced and sensitive manner relative to the pupil's age, gender, social and cultural roots. This is not to say that your views and opinions as the teacher should not be made clear, but rather that they should be part of a constructively critical and open approach, allied with a willingness to listen to other views.

Why issues?

Issues provide a marvellous opportunity for interesting learning for at least nine reasons:

1. they are real;
2. they are relevant;
3. they are immediate in time and space;
4. they are important (by definition);
5. they provide a clear focus and therefore a slim and purposeful enquiry;
6. children are involved in active not passive learning;
7. they encourage the development of informed opinions and an awareness of attitudes and values;

8. they encourage the development of political, economic, social and environmental perspectives;
9. they allow the involvement of 'real' people such as planners and councillors.

The justification for the use of controversial issues in the curriculum goes beyond relevance and interest. Issues should also be included in our teaching because they help to:

- develop evaluation skills in relation to written and broadcast information and the development of critical faculties within pupils;
- provide access to a range of points of view;
- enable pupils to distinguish between fact and opinion;
- underpin notions of freedom, tolerance, fairness, respect for truth and respect for reasoning;
- sharpen awareness of diversity of interest and motive;
- equip pupils with the skills and knowledge to seek solutions to conflict;
- enable pupils to find and accept compromise.

Approaches to issues

Curriculum Matters 7: Geography from 5 to 16 (DES 1989a) identifies twelve questions to help structure an issue-based enquiry in geography. These are:

1. What appears to be the nature of the issue?
2. Which people and what places, locations and environments are involved?
3. What views are held by individuals and groups about the problem and its possible solution and how do these vary?
4. What attitudes and values appear to underlie these different views?
5. What other information do you require to investigate the issue?
6. How can this information be usefully analysed?
7. To what extent does the evidence support or contradict alternative views?
8. What are the advantages and disadvantages of alternative solutions? Who would benefit and who would lose?
9. How good is the evidence?
10. What are your own feelings about the issue? Which proposal do you favour and why?
11. What further information do you require to make a personal judgement and how might this be obtained?
12. Have you changed your mind as a result of your investigation?

Teaching strategies

An issue-based topic allows you to use a wide range of teaching and learning styles, ranging from whole class to small group and individual work. The last two are more likely to encourage a sense of cooperation, a respect for the views of others and the ability to challenge views and facts. *Inset 5-16 Environmental Education for English* (CEE 1994) suggests eight alternative teaching strategies:

1. The issue is discussed by pupils in small groups who then report back. The teacher acts as a neutral chairperson.
2. Pupils stage a piece of drama or write poems related to the issue.
3. Pupils take on roles of people with different views and present these in a debate format.
4. Guest speakers holding different points of view on an issue are invited to speak to the class.
5. Pupils use a variety of newspaper cuttings relating to a particular issue, and from these prepare a five minute talk/presentation.
6. Pupils interview local people about an issue and report their findings.
7. Pupils give a presentation on a chosen issue to the whole school.
8. Pupils undertake a questionnaire survey around the school.

Enquiring into issues

Enquiring into issues can take the following sequence:

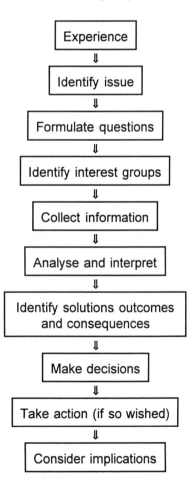

Whilst this approach may be appropriate for a detailed investigation, you may find that the following five key parts are adequate for a brief issue-based enquiry:

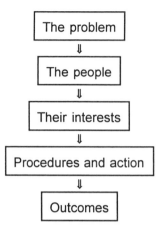

An example of this approach is described below.

The problem identified at the Annual Meeting of governors and parents of a local primary school concerns Peter's knees, Peter kept falling over in the playground and injuring his knees. This was allegedly as a result of the overcrowding of the playground shared by infants and juniors consequent upon the rapidly rising school roll. Peter's mother suggested a new playground should be built on the site of the existing school garden.

The people most involved in the issue were Peter's mother, the headteacher and a class teacher. However, a number of additional interested parties included the Local Education Authority, the Parish Priest and the writer.

Their interests ranged from a concern for Peter's safety (Peter's mother), to the Headteacher's concern for cost, legal implications and a natural concern to maintain the status quo. The class teacher, an aesthete and pragmatist, wanted the garden to be maintained as a source of beauty and contemplation and because it was a magnificent natural teaching resource.

The procedures followed to resolve this issue ranged from a parents' petition to lobbying by the School-Parents' Association, to lobbying the Governors and the Parish Priest, to writing to the local free newspaper 'Merseymart'. A range of possible solutions could be considered such as staggering playtime, using the carpark of the adjacent Parish Centre, supervising the children more closely at playtime, digging up the garden as originally suggested or doing nothing and hoping that the problem would disappear.

The outcome of this issue was that it initially disappeared under the pressure of the National Curriculum, the construction of new classrooms and the next issue, car parking outside the school in the mornings. Two years later, however, the matter has been temporarily resolved: the children are using a car park in the adjacent Parish Centre to alleviate the crowding in the school playground.

Boring local issues?

The exclusive study of global issues such as the greenhouse effect, the ozone hole and deforestation sometimes appears to preclude children's active participation. Local issues have an immediacy and relevance which makes them excellent subject matter for analysis. Also you have often only to scratch the surface of a local issue to uncover wider global connections. In a leafy suburb of Liverpool, Woolton Road is an ordinary road. Yet over a period of five years along a 400 metre stretch many opportunities have presented themselves for study by local schools. These include:

- The trees and green space versus new housing debate which arises continually.
- Building a new hotel on a 100 year old bowling green.
- The location and movement of a zebra crossing.
- The locating of a take-away 'chippy' in an ex-hardware store.
- The wearing away of the grass verge.
- The enlargement of an electricity substation.
- A traffic accident danger spot.

The following guidelines on using a local issue for environmental enquiry have been used in the study of limestone quarrying in the Peak District National Park:

- Involve students directly in enquiry into issues and decision-making systems which are of current local relevance and concern.
- Choose issues which enable consideration of official policies and plans alongside the values and opinions of other 'non-official' groups and individuals.
- In controversial issues explore all viewpoints as far as possible.
- Include the direct experience of local environments, local people and local decision-making bodies.
- Use role-play, simulation, interviewing and discussion during the work.
- Encourage a wide variety of individual student responses to environments and situations.
- Consider the scope for follow-up activity in environmental issues beyond the classroom.

Issues through stories

Fairy tales, legends, myths, stories, nursery rhymes and songs are some of the most powerful and persuasive means of bringing the environment alive to children. The use of such resources for primary age children allows them to conceptualise about places and issues beyond their immediate experience. They often produce vivid and compelling images and encourage the development of empathy and a willingness to become involved in other people's problems and issues.

Using *Bear Hunt* by Anthony Browne (Scholastic) an infant teacher developed children's mapping skills, generated a discussion of an environmental issue, animal hunting, and developed the children's understanding of a complex environmental issue.

Two hunters were trying to catch a bear, but every time they come too near he escapes in a very clever way!

- One day bear went for a walk.
- Two hunters were hunting
- They saw bear
- Look out! Look out! Bear!
- Quickly bear began to draw (a trip wire to trip the hunter)
- Well done, bear!
- But there was another hunter
- Run, bear, run!
- Out came bear's pencil (and draws a giant rhinoceros to distract the hunter)
- And bear walked on.
- Stop, the hunter's back ...
- Swiftly bear got to work (and draws again ...)
- Look up bear! (where a cage is about to drop on bear)
- Bear is caught
- But bear still has his pencil ... (and draws a saw to cut the way out)

... bear continues to evade the hunter by a cunning use of the pencil, following a route through the forest.

The children were asked to draw a range of different environments on the bear's route. This was then extended and the story used to develop and reinforce the children's map work. Finally, and possibly most valuably, the children were involved in discussions about the environmental issues associated with animal hunting.

There are many other stories, guides and compendia which may be used for such purposes including those by Anne Gadsden (1991), Brian Moses (1992a,b) and Heather Norris Nicholson (1994). Appendix 1 (page 53) contains a small selection of children's environmental fiction.

Working with people from the community

People from the community are a valuable resource in environmental education. They are real (unlike teachers who are somehow different!) and have a vast array of skills and interests. At the very least they are an extra pair of eyes and hands. At best, they offer expertise, enthusiasm, up to date information and skills from the real world, together with different perspectives on environmental issues and policy.

Levels of involvement

There are four levels of involvement possible:

1. **Communication** where teachers seek examples to support a scheme of work already determined. For example a planner or developer may be contacted and asked to provide maps and plans for a proposed new hypermarket on the edge of town.

2. **Consultation** where teachers seek comments from industrialists or others in the community on a draft teaching scheme. For example where the Planning Department agrees to comment on a scheme of work relating to land use conflicts in the local community or where the Environmental Health Department is asked to advise on how children might measure pollution and to show how the department takes its own readings.

3. **Collaboration** where teachers work with representatives of industry or the community to plan a teaching scheme. For example a local retired industrialist spends three hours per week with a group of teachers to plan a teaching scheme on the new industrial estate and arrange factory visits and interviews.

4. **Participation** where there is full participation in the planning and execution of a project. For example, representatives of local environmental pressure groups become involved in a debate about green issues or advise on conservation in the local town and also agree to take part in a role play exercise with the pupils. Alternatively parents may take over the fund raising, design and construction of projects at greatly reduced prices (not always educationally the preferred process).

Parents are a particular group of educators who can bring great improvements to the teaching programme. They know the children, the school and the area. They are committed to the school not just to the organisation they represent. They are an invaluable resource.

At St Anne's RC Infant School in Liverpool, Kathy followed a local history course co-funded by the Workers Educational Association and the Parents School Partnership. A year later she was leading the weekly Local History walk for the year 1 class; two years later she was showing the walk to student teachers.

At nearby Matthew Arnold County Primary School a parent with three children in the school has taken over the neglected school garden and now, with the help of year 4 children, has converted it into a grassy and bushy haven in the city. It is now a resource used for nature study, story time and playtime. Previously it was a depository for syringes, bottles and other debris.

Problems

Not all adult inputs are successful and you should be aware of certain difficulties associated with using adults other than teachers:

- Many are inaudible, and, if audible, boring.
- Some find it difficult to work at the children's level of comprehension and are oblivious of this fact.
- Most adopt didactic factual transmission models of delivery, full of facts but with little attention to skills, attitudes and enquiry.
- Some are delegated to attend rather than be there of their own volition, and lack enthusiasm. Others are evangelical in their enthusiasm, particularly those from large campaigning organisations.
- Some are economical with the truth and others are only au fait with information as far as the prepared text. In issue-based activities they are likely to have been enlisted because of their involvement in the issue. Their point of view may be biased.
- Many people have a tunnel view of their task and are unable to adapt to the special unique needs of individual visitor groups. Each group receives the same activities and information.

Notwithstanding these potential problems, you should bear in mind the following pointers for success when using adults:

- Aim for an experience which is mutually beneficial.
- Make sure that people from the community are adequately briefed and debriefed.
- Do not expect them to be teachers, be prepared to play devil's advocate or the village simpleton when necessary and always try to summarise or repeat key points. Always forewarn speakers that you will do this; otherwise they may see the helpful teacher as a threat!
- Try to achieve a consensus on aims beforehand.
- Wherever possible, involve them in the planning, teaching and evaluation processes.

Values and attitudes

Both enquiry and issue based learning in environmental education involve the development of values and attitudes as well as knowledge and understanding. The viewpoints, opinions and values people hold influence their reactions to environmental issues, their decisions and actions. Enquiry and issue-based learning helps children clarify their values and their roles in environmental decision-making.

Values are those ideas which a person believes to be worthwhile and which guide their thinking, communication and behaviour. They are based on the beliefs and attitudes developed as a result of interaction with family, peers, teachers, newspapers, television, radio, religion, politicians and workmates. Ethics are moral principles or rules of conduct based upon values, and they form the basis for many actions. Values form an all-embracing framework within which particular events and choices are considered.

Approaches to values development

The emphasis in values teaching is not the development of certain values but rather on the use of the valuing process. In general five methods are used.

Laissez-faire

This approach is based upon the notion that the more environmental knowledge pupils have the 'better' developed are their values.

Inculcation

Here some traditional approaches involving moralising, role modelling and inspirational stories are used to inculcate good environmental ethics and practice. These form the basis of the hidden and informal curriculum, much traditional religious education and many key stage 1 stories. In addition rules, laws and codes of practice may also have some degree of inculcation, especially where the rationale for such laws is not made explicit. Enforced action for the environment, such as compulsory 'litter picks', are similar.

Values analysis

This scientific analytical approach breaks issues and decisions down into small logical steps. The basic concept is analysed, the consequences of various actions predicted, facts are collected, the truth is assessed and relevant values are stated. A typical example of this is where a range of sites for a new reservoir are evaluated using a number of physical, economic, human and political criteria. With this approach the values underpinning each choice are made apparent by the nature of the decision reached. This approach assumes that decisions are always based upon rational, logical argument and denies intuitive subjective approaches. It also denies the opportunity to challenge the basic premise, of whether the reservoir is needed at all.

Moral reasoning

Moral growth is seen as cognitive and developmental and therefore can be developed by practising making moral decisions. Such a method involves using the unfinished moral dilemma technique where pupils are given the start of an environmental dilemma involving conflict and moral choices and then asked what should be done. For example, a town planner may be asked to recommend the preferred site for an industrial estate. The best site, which is near the railway and motorway intersection, is within sight of a high class residential suburb, his own house and that of the Mayor. The alternative is close to poor housing and will involve heavy traffic passing residential property. The Mayor's estate company has a stake in this site. What should be done?

Values clarification

Here pupils are encouraged to identify their own and others value systems. Then they are asked to publicly affirm these values and communicate them openly and honestly with others. An example of this sort of approach was used with European student teachers where an 'enviro-values continuum' exercise was used. A range of (intentionally) provocative statements (see below) were read to them and they were asked to take up positions along a single straight line extending from one end of the room to the other according to whether they agreed or disagreed with the statement.

Enviro-values continuum statements

1. The French obsession for nuclear power is dangerous to the world and should be stopped now.
2. Birth control is a valid method of solving the world's population problem.
3. The Norwegians have no right to tell the British how to run their power stations.
4. There should be a compulsory fine of £25 for all dog owners who allow their dogs to foul the pavements and grass verges.
5. The Germans should forget about the Olympics and spend the money on environmental improvements in the former East Germany.
6. Everyone has the right to smoke cigarettes in a minibus.
7. The economic benefits of tourism in the Greek Islands are outweighed by the effects on their country and traditions.

Action learning

Problem solving in real life situations in the community, not the classroom, is the basis of action learning. Here it is believed that involvement in real issues gives true insight into the hard choices that have to be made and the compromises which are often necessary. Values clarification and analysis follows later.

Teaching and learning methods

Developing values and attitudes in environmental education has implications for teaching and learning methods. In other words, 'the medium is the message'. You need to use stimulating resources as the starting point for an investigation, in order to capture children's interest and encourage them to raise questions and to share ideas. Activities which involve pupils in their own exploration of an issue are useful; for example, working in groups to produce a summary of discussion points based on a newspaper article. Role-plays and simulations can help children to explore their own environmental values and those of others, and to identify links between values and actions. Enquiry, research and the ability to present information in a meaningful manner are important skills to develop.

Environmental attitudes

Environmental attitudes are those beliefs which when focused on a specific issue or situation predispose us to act in a particular way. There are as many ideas about desirable environmental attitudes as there are environmental philosophers. The following list (CCW 1992) reflects current thinking:

- a sense of curiosity and wonder about people and the wider world;
- respect for the attitudes and values of other people and various cultural groups concerning the environment;
- an aesthetic appreciation of the natural and made environment;
- a sense of personal responsibility for the environment, locally and globally;
- a concern for the present and future quality of life of all people, flora and fauna;
- a commitment to action for just and sustainable development for all;
- a critical and discerning attitude towards opinions and policies on environmental issues;
- a readiness to evaluate and possibly modify one's own lifestyle and perspectives on environmental issues;
- a willingness to co-operate with other people in problem solving, decision-making and responding to environmental and (related) social problems;
- tolerance of uncertainty and recognition that there are no easy or final solutions to environmental problems;
- confidence in one's own ability to contribute in various ways to caring for and improving the environment.

Aesthetics, senses and feelings

As the Curriculum Council for Wales states 'environmental education is often at its most powerful when it is approached through the arts and humanities' (CCW 1992). The 1991 Geography National Curriculum made reference to fostering children's 'sense of wonder at the beauty of the world around them', and now there is the requirement in geography for children to 'express views on the attractive and unattractive features' of an environment (NCC 1995). *Curriculum Guidance 7* (NCC 1990c) stresses the value of English, art, music and drama in developing aesthetic appreciation of the environment and in offering the opportunity to understand the design aspects of the environment and the conflicts which can arise between aesthetic, utilitarian and economic considerations.

For many, awareness of the quality of the environment is the first step along the road to respect and action for the environment. In some urban areas in particular the immediate environment of the school and of many children's homes may be seen as of very poor quality, and here you will need to tread very carefully.

Sensory activities

The development of senses is routine in the primary classroom, and the natural environment provides the perfect opportunity for such activities. The traditional nature trail with its regular stops to look!, listen! and smell! has long been part of the primary teacher's repertoire. This is acknowledged in *Curriculum Guidance 7* (NCC 1990c), in a case study of a nature trail involving a blindfolded walk, with touches by the hands and feet, smells, sounds of different ground surfaces and an open area. This sort of sensory awareness and enhancement has been developed further by Steve Van Matre, an American ex-ecology professor, who has been largely responsible for the growth of Earth Education. His exhortation to 'aim for knowledge in both the head and the heart' (Van Matre 1979) summarises the central feature of his approach, the integration of the intellect and feelings. His major contribution has been to devise exciting learning experiences for young children set in an ecologically and pedagogically sound and conceptually-based context. He advocates:

Structuring by: creating magical learning experiences
focusing on sharing and doing
emphasising rewards, reinforcement and relating
and not: naming and labelling
talking without a focal point
playing twenty questions
drifting into activity entropy

Immersing in: lots of rich, first hand contact with nature

and Relating: by providing individuals with time to be alone in natural settings where they can reflect upon all life.

Whilst all of van Matre's activities should be moulded into coherent learning packages, a number of them have been widely used individually by practitioners for sensory development and enhancement. Most famous are his *Colour Chips* and *Touches*. In the former, a magical story concerning the breakage of a rainbow into millions of colours is transformed into a colour identification and matching activity as the children hunt the environment for the perfect colour match with the rainbow fragments given to each child. In *Touches*, half dozen sized egg boxes, each labelled on their underside with one set of opposite texture words such as hard and soft, rough and smooth, wet and dry, are distributed to groups of children. The activity is then divided into two parts, firstly the group have to fill one side of the box with natural items corresponding to one of the adjectives and the other side with the contrasting objects, and then secondly, the groups exchange boxes and attempt to identify the appropriate word without looking at the labels.

Other similar activities abound, including the use of map-sticks and songlines to represent a local walk (Manchester City Council, 1991). In this exercise 'useful bits' collected on a walk are tied to a stick by coloured wool in the correct geographical sequence, and using colours which reflect the feelings of the person or the state of the weather or time of day. Another way to record the journey may be in the form of a songline where different sounds reflect different parts of the stick. Another approach is that used in *Schoolbase Geography* (Scoffham *et al.* 1986) where children are asked to assess buildings and parts of buildings using 'First Impressions' and 'Different Places' worksheets which utilise checklists and opposite word charts (see worksheet on page 44). The Tidy Britain Group (Stephenson and Mares 1992) has a series of sensory walks where pupils are asked to assess the quality of places on a local walk in terms of good and bad feelings, looks, sounds and smells. This is similar to nice and nasty trails in which pupils are asked to assess pre-determined locations or make their own selections. At a more sophisticated level the ideas of the *Art and the Built Environment* Schools Council Project (Adams and Ward 1988) still have much to offer through the linking of art, architecture and environmental education.

Different places

1. Different places have different atmospheres. Walk round your school and describe in a few words how you feel about each of the places you visit. Here are some suggestions.

smelly musty frightening fun daunting clean exciting

noisy friendly gloomy dirty draughty cosy

cramped shut in comfortable quiet colourful bright

your classroom ....

a corridor ....

outside the headteacher's room ....

the cloakroom ....

the toilets ....

the library ....

the hall ....

the playground ....

the playing fields ....

2. Think of some special or unusual place (which is not mentioned in the list) where you could go if you were playing hide-and-seek. Write down where it is. Draw it in the *window* below and write some words describing it in the *shutters* on either side.

My special place is ....

Source: Scoffham *et al.* (1986).

Developing a school policy

There are three stages in the production of an environmental education policy:

1. The recognition of the **need** for an environmental education policy.
2. The **school audit**.
3. The environmental education **policy** statement.

The need

You may decide that your school needs an environmental policy for pragmatic or altruistic reasons. Pragmatically, the National Curriculum includes environmental education as a cross-curricular theme; 'green' or at least 'environmentally friendly' schools may be at an advantage in recruiting pupils; and finally, as the Association for Science Education states (1990) ' ... [environmental education] will make science more popular'. Altruistically, it may be the commitment of all or some of the staff, preferably not just the headteacher or the co-ordinator, to an environmental policy which gives powerful impetus to the greening of the school.

Cheshire County Council (Stoker 1992) have identified four areas of concern for aspiring green schools:

* the role models of the teachers and support staff;
* classroom practice and curriculum;
* other collective efforts;
* the school as an operational unit.

The production and ongoing review of the policy for environmental education should involve all pupils, staff (academic and support) and governors. It should enable pupils, parents and others in the local community to become aware of the importance and significance of environmental education both to the individual school, and the local and global community. However, the most important measure of the value of a policy lies in how effectively it is put into practice, by individual teachers and by the school as a whole. It is the reality not the rhetoric which counts!

The school audit

The school audit, familiar to all teachers since the advent of the National Curriculum, is different for environmental education, in that it goes beyond the audit of academic content to include the lifestyle of the teacher role model and the management and ethos of the school. Hence it includes:

* what and how the school teaches;
* how the school is managed to demonstrate caring for the environment

locally and globally;
- the quality of the school environment and its imaginative use and creative development.

The aim of the audit is to:

- emerge with a school policy on environmental education; and
- assess the success of the existing policy to see if it needs modification.

It is the means of identifying the match between the aims and values your school wishes to develop (the school policy) and the academic, social and physical environment in which the children learn.

The National Association for Environmental Education (Baczala 1992) has produced guidelines which include the following institutional questions:

- How is the school encouraging environmental education?
- How is environmental education managed?
- Is the school developing documentation?
- What evidence is there for integration?
- How do pupils perceive the relevance of environmental education?
- What arrangements are there for fieldwork?
- What arrangements are there for assessment?
- Is the school estate used as a learning resource?
- What arrangements are there for the management of the school estate?
- To what extent does the school manage its own environment?

The Royal Society for the Protection of Birds (Elcombe 1991) and Cheshire County Council (Stoker 1992) have both produced detailed checklists which focus on school management and ethos with respect to environmental impact. Dorion (1993) identifies seven areas for environmental audit, including the use of energy, management of waste, purchasing policy, use of transport, use of resources in the classroom, management of school grounds and the management of cleaning and caretaking. The Council for Environmental Education (1992) has put forward a list of questions to assist schools in developing a school policy and guidelines for environmental education. At a very practical level the National Association for Environmental Education has produced a collection of simple ideas to help teachers implement environmental approaches to the whole curriculum (Baczala 1994). Pike and Selby (1990) combine both environmental and educational dimensions in their Charter for green schools (see below). The Charter offers a checklist covering the four elements which the authors see as essential for a green school, namely curriculum entitlement to environmental education, equal opportunities, eco-friendliness and empowering ethos.

46

Charter for a green school

Entitlement curriculum	Comments	Action needed
1. Does your written policy (and prospectus) clearly state your aims and objectives for environmental education?		
2. Do you have effective co-ordination of environmental education as a cross-curricular theme?		
3. Are you taking every opportunity to introduce environmental education into all core and other foundation subjects?		
4. Are you ensuring appropriate progression and continuity for environmental education throughout the school?		
5. Are you actively engaged in corporate evaluation of your environmental education provision?		
Equal Opportunities 6. Is the prevailing ethos of the school and the curriculum, including the environmental education programme, sensitive to issues of gender equality?		
7. Does the prevailing ethos of the school and the curriculum, including the environmental education programme, adequately prepare students for life in a multicultural society?		
8. Are special needs of all kinds considered by both staff and students and actively catered for?		
9. Are the diverse learning needs of the student population met by a varied diet of teaching and learning approaches across the curriculum?		
10. Have all staff, irrespective of specialism, been engaged in professional development so they are equally able to deliver the entitlement curriculum?		

Entitlement curriculum	Comments	Action needed
Eco-friendliness 11. Does your school use recycled materials whenever possible and have an active and throughgoing recycling policy?		
12. Does your school actively promote and practice energy efficiency?		
13. Does your school purchase and use resources with a view to minimising harm to the planet?		
14. Do your school buildings and surroundings provide an aesthetically pleasing environment in which to live and learn?		
15. Does your school actively promote health-enhancing attitudes and behaviours amongst both staff and students?		
Empowering ethos 16. Does your school place a premium on fostering humane personal relationships grounded in the enhancement of self-esteem and mutual regard?		
17. Are staff and students rights respected and is the opportunity given for them to contribute to decision-making processes?		
18. Are students given the opportunities and skills to participate constructively in helping to safeguard their environment?		
19. Does the school play an active role in the community and the community in the school?		
20. Does the prevailing ethos of the school demonstrate that people matter and that everyone has a contribution to make to social and environmental improvement?		

Source: Pike and Selby (1990).

At the academic level a standard audit form relating curriculum knowledge statements, skills and attitudes and values to each year of school, or to each subject is commonplace (Dorion 1993) as are simpler matrices relating topics in, about and for the environment to knowledge and understanding, attitudes and values and skills.

School policies

The aim of a school audit is to produce a workable policy which ensures the place of environmental education in your school curriculum. Whilst every school will have its own specific policy, you can learn much from the experiences of other schools. In the Shropshire County Council guide to environmental education the following sample entry for a school prospectus is included.

Respecting the environment

We are committed as a school to developing the widest possible awareness of environmental issues. Education about worldwide issues related to protecting and respecting the environment has its place in the curriculum in science, technology, humanities and personal and social education.

It is important that our children are aware on a day to day basis of environmental issues in their lives. We discourage unnecessary waste of materials and we are particularly concerned that pupils are conscious of the problem of litter. We encourage all pupils to make their contribution to keeping our site free from litter. As a whole school we aim to play our part in promoting environmental awareness throughout our community.

You may be able to adapt this succinct statement to the particular needs of your own school.

At Snodland CEP School the following nine point school environmental charter is in operation (Baczala 1992).

At all times the pupils, staff and friends of Snodland CEP School will try to:

1. keep the school grounds clear of litter;
2. save energy by switching off unwanted lights and heaters and keeping doors and windows closed;
3. recycle as much as possible, ranging from cans to stamps;
4. use environmentally friendly cleaning materials;
5. use recycled paper products;
6. develop and improve the school grounds and plant more trees;
7. keep the school a non-smoking zone;
8. not waste natural resources like food and water;
9. teach everyone about the importance of caring for our environment.

The logical next step is the production of a school Environmental Education Policy.

Ankermoor Primary School in Staffordshire has had such a policy since 1990. The description below demonstrates the beneficial effect that environmental education can have on values, attitudes, and most importantly, on actions, when it is incorporated by the whole school as a dimension to learning.

Ankermoor Primary School's environmental education policy has a wide variety of aims including the promotion of:

- *the development of well balanced and healthy people;*
- *a caring attitude;*
- *a commitment to personal involvement;*
- *a positive approach to conservation and green issues.*

Consequent upon this they have identified a number of issues for attention which include litter, recycling, paper purchase, wooden items, aerosols and cleaning agents, the tuck shop, healthy eating, energy conservation, school grounds and in-service training.

Litter is seen as an individual as well as a social responsibility. Litter picks have been so successful that the activity is no longer required! A 'waste not, want not' philosophy prevails and recycled materials are used in art and technology. Jumble and nearly-new sales are held regularly and composting is an integral part of the development. Bulk paper purchasing of a minimum of different items to reduce waste is practised as is the purchase of recycled paper. Wooden items are acquired from 'properly harvested and suitable' woods. With regards to aerosols and cleaning agents, environmentally friendly items are used wherever possible, although a price premium on recycled products and the bulk purchasing policy of the LEA from a narrow range of suppliers have not helped. The school tuck shop is run as a mini enterprise with profits donated to school funds. Healthy foods are researched and, in conjunction with the school kitchen service, the understanding and practice of good eating habits is promoted. Energy and water conservation for economic and environmental reasons is practised and studied within the curriculum. The school grounds are seen as a proper concern for the wider school community and offer opportunities for the development of caring attitudes and a sense of ownership. Finally in-service training takes a whole school approach, and includes environmental considerations.

Bibliography

Adams, E. and Ward, C. (1988)
Art and the Built Environment,
Schools Council.

Association for Science Education (1990)
Opening Doors for Science,
ASE and Nature Conservancy Council.

Baczala, K. (1992)
Towards a School Policy for Environmental Education: Environmental Audit, NAEE.

Baczala, K. (1994)
Positive Action, NAEE.

Billimore, B., *et al* (1990)
The Outdoor Classroom, DES/HMSO.

Birmingham City Council (1992)
Environmental Learning Across the Curriculum, Birmingham City Council.

Copeland, T. (1993)
A Teacher's Guide to Geography and the Historic Environment, English Heritage.

Cornell, J.B. (1989)
Sharing Nature with Children, Exley.

Council for Environmental Education (1992)
Inset 5-16 Introducing Environmental Education, CEE.

CEE (1993)
Inset 5-16 Environmental Education for Science, CEE.

CEE (1994a)
Inset 5-16 Environmental Education for Geography, CEE.

CEE (1994b)
Inset 5-16 Environmental Education for English, CEE.

CEE (1995a)
Inset 5-16 Environmental Education for the Arts, CEE.

CEE (1995b)
Inset 5-16 Environmental Education for Technology, CEE.

Curriculum Council for Wales (1992)
Environmental Education: A Framework for the Development of a Cross-curricular Theme in Wales. Advisory Paper 17, CCW.

Department of Education and Science (1989a)
Curriculum Matters 7: Geography from 5-16, HMSO.

DES (1989b)
Curriculum Matters 13: Environmental Education from 5-16, HMSO.

Derbyshire County Council (1992)
A Derbyshire Approach to Environmental Education, Derbyshire CC.

Dorion, C. (1993)
Planning and Evaluation of Environmental Education, CEE/WWF UK.

Elcombe, D.M. (1991)
Environmental Education: The Vital Link, RSPB.

Gadsden, A. (1991)
Geography and History Through Stories, Geographical Association/Cheshire CC.

Hull, R. (ed.) (1991)
Green Poetry, Wayland.

Lancashire County Council (1992)
Environmental Education Guidelines 4-16, Lancashire CC.

Manchester City Council (1991)
Cross-Curricular Themes, Skills and Dimensions - Implementing the Whole Curriculum, COIC.

Manchester City Council and the Field Studies Council (1993)
Outdoor and Environmental Education, FSC.

Mares, C. and Stephenson, R. (1988)
Inside Outside, Tidy Britain Group.

Merseyside Environmental Trust/Liverpool City Council (1993) *Promoting a project,* Conference on the Environment, 1993

Moses, B. (1992a)
Catching the Light, WWF UK.

Moses, B. (1992b)
Somewhere to be: Language and the Environment, WWF UK.

National Curriculum Council (1989)
Circular Number 6, NCC.

NCC (1990a)
Curriculum Guidance 3. The Whole Curriculum, NCC.

NCC (1990b)
Curriculum Guidance 4. Education for Economic and Industrial Understanding, NCC.

NCC (1990c)
Curriculum Guidance 7. Environmental Education, NCC.

NCC (1990d)
Curriculum Guidance 8. Education for Citizenship, NCC.

NCC (1991)
EIU Managing Economic and Industrial Understanding in Schools, NCC.

NCC (1993)
Teaching Geography at Key Stages 1 and 2: An INSET Guide, NCC.

NCC (1995)
Key Stages 1 and 2 of the National Curriculum, HMSO.

Neal, P. and Palmer, J. (1990)
Environmental Education in the Primary School, Blackwell.

Norris Nicholson, H. (1994)
Place in Story-time, Geographical Association.

Northumberland County Council (undated)
Environmental Education in the Curriculum 4-19, Northumberland CC.

Phillips, A. (1993)
Environmental Education. E&D File, UN Non-Governmental Liaison Service.

Pike, G. and Selby, D. (1990)
Greening the Staffroom, Centre for Global Education/BBC Education/WWF UK.

Pirrie, J. (1994)
On Common Ground, WWF UK.

Randle, D. (1989)
Teaching Green, Green Print.

Scoffham, S., Bridge, C. and Jewson, T. (1986)
Schoolbase Geography, Schofield and Sims.

Sefton Education Authority (1994)
An Approach to Environmental Education in Sefton, Sefton LEA.

Shropshire County Council (undated)
A Guide to Developing Environmental Education in Shropshire Secondary Schools, Shropshire CC.

Stephenson, R. and Mares, C. (1992)
Environmental Education and Tomorrow's Citizen, Tidy Britain Group.

Stoker, B. (1992)
A Green Guide for Schools, Cheshire CC.

Stoker, B. and Brawn, T. (1993)
From Giant Sweets to Sponge Floors: A School Grounds Design Guide, Cheshire CC.

Van Matre, S. (1979)
Sunship Earth, Institute for Earth Education.

Worldwide Fund for Nature (1988)
A Common Purpose: Environmental Education and the School Curriculum, WWF UK.

Appendix 1: Environmental fiction

Anno, M.
All in a Day,
Hamish Hamilton (ISBN 0 241 11799 2)

Ayres, P.
When Dad Cuts Down the Chestnut Tree,
Walker (ISBN 0 7445 1436 3)

Baker, J.
Where the Forest Meets the Sea,
Julia McRae (ISBN 0 86203 317 9)

Baker, J.
Home in the Sky,
Julia McRae (ISBN 0 86203 183 4)

Bash, B.
Tree of Life: The World of the African Baobab,
Sierra Club Books/Little, Brown and Company (ISBN 0 316 88840 0)

Brown, R.
The World that Jack Built,
Andersen Press (ISBN 0 86264 269 8)

Browne, A.
Bear Hunt,
Scholastic

Burningham, J.
Oi! Get off our Train,
Cape (ISBN 0 22402 698 4)

Cartwright, A. and R.
The Last Dodo,
Hutchinson (ISBN 0 09962 230 0)

Corbett, W.J.
Toby's Iceberg,
Methuen

Cowcher, H.
Rainforest,
Andre Deutsch (ISBN 0 233 93266 3)

Cowcher, H.
Antarctica,
Corgi (ISBN 0 233 98451 8)

Dupasquier, P.
Our House on the Hill,
Puffin (ISBN 0 14 050781 7)

Foreman, M.
Dinosaurs and All that Rubbish,
Puffin (ISBN 0 14 050098 7)

Foreman, M.
One World,
Andersen Press (ISBN 0 86264 289 2)

Gates, S.
Dragline,
Oxford (ISBN 0 19 271663 8)

Glimmerveen, U.A.
A Tale of Antarctica,
Scholastic (ISBN 0 590 76361 X)

Harranth, W. and Opgenorth, W.
Isn't it a Beautiful Meadow,
Oxford (ISBN 0 19 279815 4)

Husband T. and Wood, D.
Save the Human,
Antelope Books, Hamish Hamilton

James, S.
My Friend Whale,
Walker (ISBN 0 7445 1500 9)

James, S.
Dear Greenpeace,
Walker

Jones, A.
Aardvarks, disembark!,
Julia Macrae (ISBN 1 85681 000 3)

Keeping, C.
Adam and Paradise Island,
Oxford (ISBN 0 19 279842 1)

Kerven, R.
Wild,
Blackie

Martinez, C.
Once Upon a Planet,
Puffin

Mayne, W.
The Farm that Ran Out of Names,
Red Fox

McNaughton, C.
Watch out for the Giant-killers,
Walker

Mounter, P.
Attila the Hen,
Yearling

Morpurgo, M.
Why the Whales Came
Heinemann (ISBN 1 434 95200 1)

Owen, G.
Never Walk Alone,
Lions

Rowlands, A.
Poll,
Oxford

Smith, A.M.
Akimbo and the Elephants,
Mammoth

Snape, J. and Snape, C.
Giant,
Walker (ISBN 0 7445 1441 X)

Weller, F.W.
I Wonder if I'll See a Whale,
Hodder and Stoughton
(ISBN 0 340 54665 4)

Wiseman, D.
Adam's Common
Corgi

Appendix 2: Useful addresses

Association for Science Education, College Lane, Hatfield, Herts AL10 9AA.

British Ecological Society, Burlington House, Piccadilly, London W1V 0LG.

Association for Agriculture, Victoria Chambers, 16-20 Strutton Ground, London SW1 2HP.

British Trust for Conservation Volunteers, 36 St Mary's Street, Wallingford, Oxfordshire OX10 0EU.

Centre for Alternative Technology, Llwyngwern Quarry, Machynlleth, Powys SY20 9AZ.

Centre for Global Education, College of Ripon and York St John, Lord Mayor's Walk, York YO3 7EX.

Civic Trust (contact for British Telecom's Environment Week), 17 Carlton House, London SW1 2HP.

Council for Environmental Education, University of Reading, London Road, Reading, Berkshire RG1 5AQ.

Council for the Protection of Rural England, Warwick House, 25 Buckingham Palace Road, London SW1 0PP.

Countryside Commission, John Dower House, Crescent Place, Cheltenham GL50 3RA.

English Heritage Education Service, Keysign House, 429 Oxford Street, London W1R 2HD.

English Nature, Northminster House, Peterborough PE1 1UA.

Field Studies Council, Central Services, Preston Montford, Montford Bridge, Shrewsbury SY4 1HW.

Friends of the Earth, 26-28 Underwood Street, London N1 7JQ.

The Geographical Association, 343 Fulwood Road, Sheffield S10 3BP.

Greenpeace, Canonbury Villas, London N1 2PN.

Green Teacher, Machynlleth, Powys SY20 8DN.

Groundwork (contact for ESSO Greenlink Project and Young Energy Savers), 85/87 Cornwall Street, Birmingham B3 3BY.

Institute of Earth Education, Ufton Court Centre, Green Lane, Nervet, Berkshire RG7 4HD.

Learning Through Landscapes Trust, Third Floor, Technology House, Victoria Road, Winchester SO23 7DU.

National Association for Environmental Education, Walsall Campus, University of Wolverhampton, Gorway, Walsall WS1 3BD.

National Association for Outdoor Education, 251 Woodlands Road, Woodlands, Southampton SO4 2GJ.

National Association for Urban Studies, The Canterbury Centre, St Alphege Lane, Canterbury CT1 2EB.

National Federation of City Farms, 93 Whitby Road, Brislington, Bristol BS4 3BR.

National Trust, 36 Queen Anne's Gate, London SW1 9AS.

Religious Education and Environment Programme (REEP), 8th Floor, Rodwell House, Middlesex Street, London E1 7HJ.

Royal Society for the Prevention of Cruelty to Animals, Causeway, Horsham, West Sussex RH12 1HG.

Royal Society for the Protection of Birds, The Lodge, Sandy, Bedfordshire SG19 2DL.

School Curriculum Industry Partnership (SCIP), Centre for Education and Industry, University of Warwick, Westwood Site, Coventry CV4 7AL.

Shell Better Britain Campaign, Red House, Hill Lane, Great Barr, Birmingham B43 6LZ.

Soil Association, British Organic Farmers, 86-88 Colston Street, Bristol BS1 5BB.

Tidy Britain Group, The Pier, Wigan, Lancashire WN3 4EX.

Town and Country Planning Association, 17 Carlton House Terrace, London SW1Y 5AS.

WATCH Trust for Environmental Education, The Green, Witham Park, Lincoln LN5 7JR.

Wildlife and Wetlands Trust, Slimbridge, Gloucestershire GL2 7BT.

WorldAware, Regent's College, Inner Circle, Regent's Park, London NW1 4NS.

World Wide Fund for Nature (WWF UK), Panda House, Weyside Park, Godalming, Surrey GU7 1XR.